Come
With Me

Don,
Thank you for making space in your life for me. For "speaking to my face with your face". You encourage and challenge me in profound ways and I am hugely grateful!
Elaine.

Discovery House Publishers

Books, music, and videos that feed the soul with the Word of God

Box 3566 Grand Rapids, MI 49501

COME

WITH ME

*An invitation to break
through the wall
between you and God*

ELAINE MARTENS HAMILTON
AND KATHY ESCOBAR

Come with Me
©2002 by Elaine Martens Hamilton and Kathy Escobar
All rights reserved.

Discovery House Publishers is affiliated with RBC Ministries,
Grand Rapids, Michigan 49512.

Discovery House books are distributed to the trade exclusively by
Barbour Publishing, Inc., Uhrichsville, Ohio 44683.

Unless otherwise indicated, all Scripture quotations are from
The New International Version (NIV), © 1973, 1978, 1984 by the
International Bible Society. Used by permission of Zondervan Bible
Publishers, Grand Rapids, Michigan.

Library of Congress Cataloging-in-Publication Data
Hamilton, Elaine Martens
    Come with me : an invitation to break through the wall between you
and God / Elaine Martens Hamilton, Kathy Escobar.
    p. cm.
ISBN: 1-57293-071-3
1. Christian women—Religious life. I. Escobar, Kathy. II. Title.
BV4527.H345 2002
248.8'43—dc21   2002001396

Printed in the United States of America
02 03 04 05 06 07 08 09 / DP / 9 8 7 6 5 4 3 2 1

To my parents, Peter and Johanna Martens,
who taught me about faith and perseverance.
Because of you, I have never known a day without an
awareness of God's presence. Thank you. I love you.
Elaine

To my faithful husband and closest friend. Your love,
your inspiration, your laughter have carried me through.
You are the joy of my heart.

And to my kids—Josh, Julia, Jamison, Jonas, and Jared.
Through each of you, I get a beautiful glimpse
of God's love for me.
With love, Kathy

Contents

Prologue ~ 9

One
Come with Me ~ 19

Two
God Loves Us, Not Our Performance ~ 37

Three
God Wants to Connect Intimately with Us ~ 65

Four
God Is Working on Our Behalf ~ 81

Five
God Will Always Be Faithful to Us ~ 99

Six
God Believes in Who He Created Us to Be ~ 123

Seven
God Will Continue to Pursue Us ~ 137

Prologue

Not Like Other Lovers

Many years ago, a kind and gentle king ruled over the small village where Dara and her family lived. He and his family were dearly loved by the people. Previous rulers had been oppressive, heavily taxing the people and forcing many into servitude. But now the villagers lived without fear, and the town square was often filled with laughter. Even difficult times were more easily borne because the people knew their troubles would not escape the king's attention. He could often be found visiting those in need to give a word of encouragement or a gift to alleviate their distress.

Rumor had it that the king had decided to select a commoner for his heir, the prince, to marry when he came of age. The king confirmed this one day at a ball given in honor of the prince's fifth birthday. He announced that he wished for his son to wed a young woman from within his kingdom. In this way he could ensure that the prince would rule with a clearer understanding of the needs of his subjects. The people were thrilled at the news. Never before had there been an opportunity for a commoner to marry into the royal family. For many months after the ball the people spoke of nothing else. Families began to groom their young girls toward this possibility, diligently educating them in matters of protocol and etiquette.

Dara's family was particularly hopeful. Their daughter was a beautiful and engaging child. The king had said so himself on one of his visits to the family's home. Dara's parents felt they had a better chance than most since the king had already noticed her. Many hours were spent teaching Dara the proper ways of a princess. As a child, she loved the attention and enjoyed the dream of someday becoming a princess. But as she grew older, the dream became a heavy burden. There were never-ending corrections and criticisms, constant reprimands—she wasn't walking like a princess, she wasn't eating like a princess, a princess would never have said that, a princess would have studied more thoroughly. The list went on and on. Every accomplished skill led to another task. And she was always aware that she was not alone in the quest to be chosen. So many girls in the village were vying for the prince's attention. The tension among them sometimes led to arguments over who was most suited for the prince. Though she had learned much about proper manners, hosting parties, and what was required of the wife of a prince, she found herself wondering what real chance she had to be chosen. There were other young girls who were more accomplished and attractive than she was. Could she possibly be enough to capture the heart of a prince?

Time passed and she was now of marrying age, but there had been no word from the king regarding his selection. Dara grew convinced that her efforts were now futile. It seemed that the only sensible thing to do was to give up the pursuit and find a mate of her own station. So Dara turned her attention to the young men in the village.

One young man began to fill her daydreams. He was the son of a wealthy farmer, a friend of her father's. They did not know each other well, but the longer she observed him the more desperate she became to win his affections.

He did not make the pursuit easy for her. In the beginning he seemed thrilled with her attention. Days were filled with pleasures and amusements they enjoyed together. But some days he toyed with her, pretending he was no longer interested in her. Yet inevitably the game would be followed with a shower of attention and flowers. Initially her parents objected and tried to persuade her to wait and see if the king might still choose her, but she convinced them that her chances were slim and that after waiting she might be left without any husband. Besides, her suitor was successful and admired in the village. There was no need to worry; they would have a wonderful life together. He meant everything to her. Finally her parents gave their blessing, and the young man proposed, presenting her with a beautiful ring. It had been a challenge to capture his heart, and now knowing she had won him filled her completely.

But as plans for the wedding celebration proceeded, something began to change. She was no longer sure that he was only pretending to be disinterested in her at times. He seemed constantly restless, sometimes moody and irritable. He rarely laughed at her jokes now or gazed at her the way he used to. More and more he left her behind, choosing to pursue his pleasures in the company of his old friends. When she questioned him, he dismissed her concerns, saying only that he was trying to enjoy his last days of youth before he took on the responsibilities of a wife. She was terribly hurt by his response but reasoned that he was only nervous about the wedding and needed for her to be more attentive.

She did everything she could think of to rouse his affection for her. She dressed and spoke in ways she thought would please him. She threw elaborate parties, serving choice wines and special dishes. She flattered and praised him and catered to his every whim. But nothing moved him. She begged him to tell her what she could do to make him happy again. She told him she was willing to do anything because of her love for him. This angered him, and he sent her away, saying she was being tiresome, expecting too much from their relationship. Not long afterwards he broke their engagement, announcing that she was not what he had expected and that he had been bored with her for quite some time.

Her grief and humiliation were overwhelming. In her sadness she took to walking in the woods at the far end of the village. It was peaceful there. No one bothered her; no one saw her tears. It was there, in those hours alone, that she resolved never to love again. Clearly she was not enough to capture a man's heart, and she would not be hurt again by giving herself to another.

One day as she wandered there, she encountered a nobleman. She was startled, but his kind voice put her at ease.

"I have come as a friend," he said. "I have seen you here among the trees many times. I have often wanted to talk with you. But you looked as though you wished to be alone. I have come today because I could not stop myself. Why do you cry here so often? What has wounded you so?"

She looked at the ground for a moment before she answered. "Love," she said.

"Love?" he asked. "What kind of love could lead to such pain? Tell me who has hurt you."

Touched by his concern, her story began to tumble out—about her attempt to win the prince and the rejection of the farmer's son. "I was such a fool!" she said, after she had told him all that had happened. "I believed in fairy-tale love and happily-ever-afters. But I am not a child anymore. I have learned much since then."

The stranger listened quietly, saying nothing. But she was surprised to see tears in his eyes. He asked if they could meet again the next day and talk some more.

After that, they met often in the forest. He seemed keenly interested in her thoughts and asked her opinion about everything. Some days they talked of inconsequential things—recent happenings in the village, friends they had in common. Other days they talked of more painful things—of love and commitment. He spoke of loyalty and devotion as if he truly believed in them. She told him over and over that love was too dangerous, that she would not allow it to hurt her again. One day he pressed her, asking what value life had without passion and romance. She had tried to be careful not to offend him, but now she was angry.

"Passion and romance are just part of the fairy tale! They are not real! They are lies! I am not enough for anyone to love forever!" It seemed to her that he had no right to ask such questions. What was his purpose in talking to her so? It was as if he intended to awaken the longings that had led to her disaster.

"Leave me alone," she cried. "I do not wish to speak of this again. I am done with love."

She turned to go, but he reached out for her.

"It is time for me to tell you," he said. "I am the prince. A bride was never selected for me. My father freed me to choose on my own, and I have chosen you."

She was stunned! "Why would you want me when there are so many others better suited for you than I?"

"When I saw your pain, I knew that you could love deeply, that you were real. The others only pretend at love. I have been waiting to find someone who would share her heart with me. I chose you that first day I saw you here in the woods. I never spoke of it until now because I did want to frighten or obligate you."

"What if I cannot believe you?" she asked.

"Then I will pursue you until you can."

"You will only be disappointed with me as others have been."

"I am not like other lovers," he said. "You are enough for me."

She studied him now. "How can I know that you will be true?"

"You cannot know until you let me show you. There is so much I long to give you."

Crying, she covered her face with her hands. "I fear I need so much more than I can ever have from love."

He took her hands in his. "My beloved, come with me. I am not afraid of your desperation. I am strong enough to love you, and I will not give you up."

"But then I will win her back once again. I will lead her out into the desert and speak tenderly to her there. I will return her vineyards to her and transform the Valley of Trouble into a gateway of hope. She will give herself to me there, as she did long ago when she was young, when I freed her from her captivity in Egypt. In that coming day," says the Lord, "you will call me 'my husband' instead of 'my master.'" (HOSEA 2:14–16, NEW LIVING TRANSLATION)

"How can I give you up . . . ? How can I hand you over . . . ? . . . For I am God, and not man."
HOSEA 11:8–9

Journaling

Write about how some of your experiences with a parent, boyfriend/ spouse, or friend have left you wanting, disappointed, or confused.

_____

_____

_____

_____

_____

_____

_____

_____

_____

_____

_____

_____

_____

_____

Are there some ways in which you are holding back because you are afraid God might not be able or willing to give you all that you need from Him? Write about that.

_____

_____

Small-Group Discussion Questions

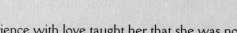

Dara's experience with love taught her that she was not enough to capture the heart of another. She tried everything she knew to please him, but all her efforts were inadequate.

- ❧ Talk about how you relate to the story, perhaps to the idea of needing to perform for others and for God. What thoughts or feelings came up as you read it?

- ❧ What part of the story impacted you the most?

1

Come with Me

"Come with Me."

Elaine's Experience

A few years ago I wrote this in my journal:

I need some exercise. My body feels cramped and numb. A walk will make me feel better. I head out the door and concentrate on getting my heart rate up. I've pounded out a few miles before I realize that I'm walking with my head down again. I'm watching the pavement, ticking off the miles. I'm always doing that. All around me are trees and flowers, but I've missed them. I've missed the smell of the jasmines in my neighbor's front yard. I've forgotten to look at that stunning bougainvillea at the house on the corner. I didn't notice the sound of the water in the creek where my children like to play. I've missed it all, staring at the pavement, thinking about what's next. There was so much more I could have experienced, but I'm not good at being in the moment. I do not like to be in the middle of things. I like to be finished.

I have approached my time with God the same way. I know that He is what I need, and so I try to get refreshed by spending some time with Him. But my focus is off. I race through the event, thinking of it as a task. I read a passage, answer some Bible study questions, and pray through a formula. There—done! But nothing changes. Not me, not my relationships or my attitudes. I feel like I am spinning my wheels. I'm doing what I know to do, but I am left unsatisfied.

God has been talking to me about that. He's been teaching me that He does things differently than I do. He invites me to come away with Him, to walk with Him. He says that being together is the whole point. He tells me to slow down, to listen for His voice, that He wants to talk to me. He tells me to stop looking at my watch. He says to me, "You cannot be refreshed when you are concentrating on ticking off the miles."

Too many times it seems we come away from our time alone with God with our longings to connect with Him unfulfilled. We know that He is what we need, that only His power can create the change we want or give the direction we need. So we do what we know to do. We read, we pray, we do another Bible study. But nothing much seems to happen. We hope for a more tangible awareness of His presence, a deeper sense of His working in our lives, and yet He remains inaccessible, elusive. We wonder what's wrong. Is it us? Is it Him? Or is the kind of spiritual intimacy David reveals in the Psalms available only to a select few? Is there some invisible line of maturity we have yet to reach when He will finally become accessible to us? Is His silence punishment for the failures on our part? Why can't we hear Him? Why can't we feel Him? Or does He not want to be that involved with us?

When we (Kathy and Elaine) first began to express these fears we thought we were alone in our frustration. But since then we have heard many other women express similar feelings:

- "I feel like I'm doing everything I know to do, and it's not enough. I'm reading the Bible, praying, serving in my church, but I still feel alone in my relationship with God."

- "I'm weary and confused about what it means to be a Christian woman."

- "Intellectually I believe all the right things, but it hasn't translated into much power in my life. I continually struggle with the same old things, and I can't seem to get His help. It feels as if God is just standing on the sidelines watching me struggle."

- "Honestly, I'm afraid that I'm a constant disappointment to God. I'm always trying to do something that will prove to Him that I'm serious about my faith. Maybe if I do something really big I'll feel closer to Him."

- "I know I'm supposed to feel convicted about my sin and be motivated to change, but most of the time I don't. I never seem to make much progress. I don't think I'll ever be what I should be, so I guess I've given up on trying to grow."

The more women we talked to, the clearer it became that we were all in the same boat! We were afraid that maybe all there was was what we had: an intellectual faith with sound theology and right behaviors. We looked good on the outside but were wasting away on the inside, longing for something deeper, for a way to connect with Him so that our hearts would agree with our heads about who

He is. We studied more, worked harder, but what we finally learned was that it wasn't that we didn't have enough information about *God*. The problem was that we didn't have enough information about *ourselves*.

What we discovered was that our past experiences in relationships had created barriers between us and God. When important people in our lives have been rejecting, abandoning, or dismissing, it is difficult to approach God without carrying these expectations of relationships with us. Yes, we knew that God is accepting and faithful and protecting, but having never experienced that kind of love, we were stuck expecting His love to look like the kind we had been given. It seems we had unintentionally hooked God to the pain of other relationships in our lives, secretly fearing that we couldn't find or didn't deserve true love.

We began to explore the ways in which our experiences were influencing our relationship with God, identifying distortions in our emotional responses to Him even though our intellectual understanding of Him was sound. We asked Him to show us the ways in which we were protecting ourselves from Him, holding back because we were afraid of being hurt or abandoned. And He began to tell us.

For example, I (Elaine) realized that I had a pattern of distancing myself from God whenever something good happened. In my family I received special attention from an uncle who also molested me. Good things were always followed by violation and humiliation. I learned that good things had strings attached, that there was a price to be paid. And I unintentionally carried that expectation into my relationship with God. All good things became suspect. Whenever something wonderful happened, I would initially thank God for it, but then I would withdraw from Him, with no desire to speak to Him for weeks or months. It dawned on me one day that I was waiting for the other shoe to drop. I was getting angry with God in anticipation of the humiliation I was sure would follow. When I finally realized what was happening, I asked God to find a way to teach me His true character through experiences with Him. Over time He brought a series of good things into my life, things that couldn't be explained except by His direct intervention. And I began to learn to trust His goodness, to accept and enjoy what He sends my way. I have been learning that He delights in giving good gifts to His children because that's who He really is.

I (Kathy) learned early on to cope in my broken family by staying in control of everything. I learned that love was something to be earned, and I worked hard to earn it by performing perfectly. Staying on top of everything ensured people would like me, need me, love me. If I failed them, I felt sure I would lose their love. This expectation of having to work for love spilled over into my relationship with God. Unconditional love was a theological idea, not something I'd ever experienced. While I knew the right Scriptures about grace, acceptance, and mercy, I struggled with feeling compelled to prove myself worthy of His love. But God began to teach me His true character through other people in my life. As I honestly shared my struggles with others and experienced their acceptance, I began to trust in His acceptance of me as well. These people loved me regardless of what I did for them. They loved me when I wasn't on top of things or when I made huge mistakes. They loved me even when I shared my shameful secrets and the dark corners of my heart. God worked through these people to show me that love isn't based on my performance. These experiences have made the truth of God's unconditional love for me real, alive, and life-changing.

What we hope to do with this material is to provide you with opportunities to identify and work through some of your own distortions. We want to help you remove some of the barriers that have been created so you can experience God more intimately—so you can embrace emotionally the truth you already believe intellectually. We hope you will think of this time as something you are doing for yourself—an opportunity to be comforted and nurtured, to be strengthened and directed. The questions and directions are designed to create interaction between you and God—to help you talk to God about what is deep in your heart, to help you hear His voice in response to your needs. There is no formula to follow, no right way to do this. You will find your own way to connect with Him, and He will speak to you however He chooses to.

Each of the following chapters explores various aspects of God's true character: that He is personal, intimate, and nurturing; that He unconditionally and faithfully loves; that He protects, rescues, and restores us; that He believes in and hopes for us. Within each chapter you will find women sharing their stories. (Some of you may recognize these stories from Elaine's first book, *Leave the Mud and Learn to Soar,* also by Discovery House Publishers.) They will share with you how their histories have colored their relationships with God and created fears that have limited intimacy with Him. All these women are committed Christians. Many are leaders in their churches. They are successful in many ways in their lives and are some of the most remarkable people we know. And yet, as you will see, they struggle with fears and distortions about God. From our work with women, we know that these women's stories are representative of many others. We hope their stories will help you feel less alone in your efforts to pursue a deeper relationship with God.

After each story you will find Scripture passages and questions to help you explore how you relate to different aspects of God's character. We suggest that you look up the passage in your Bible and then journal your responses to the questions in the space provided. Blank journaling pages are provided at the end of each section, so don't feel limited by thinking you can fill only the given amount of lines for each question. You may want to use a separate journal so you have plenty of space. Some of the questions will ask you to think about painful things—to explore feelings or memories you may not have verbalized before. Though it is painful and sometimes scary, we believe this is a necessary step. Write all of this to God, as if you are writing Him a letter that He is reading at the moment you are writing it.

You will be invited to ask Him to talk to you about specific issues in your life and write down what you think He may be saying in response. You may struggle with believing that God can or will speak to you. Perhaps you're afraid you are not worthy of that kind of intimacy with Him. We have found in our struggle to learn to hear Him that He is eager to communicate. What we have to do is get ready to hear Him. Hearing God's voice is a learning process that takes time and practice. But we believe it is available to everyone who desires it. You don't have to have reached some high level of spiritual maturity. You don't have to have it all together, with all the struggles of your life under control. We are living proof of that! He is available to you just as you are. The key is persistence and openness. You will need to decide if you are ready to hear Him and if you can try to trust Him to lead you through this process.

"Come with me by yourselves to a quiet place and get some rest."
MARK 6:31

We understand that this may be new for you. Try not to be discouraged if you feel as if nothing is happening. As you continue to practice listening, you will begin to hear or experience something that sounds different from your internal voice. This will take some time. We suggest giving yourself at least ten minutes to sit still, doing nothing but listening and waiting to sense His presence. Write down whatever you become aware of, whatever comes to mind. It may be a word or phrase or verse. It may be a picture He creates in your mind or a memory of an experience in the past. It may be a physical sensation. Don't get frustrated if you think you are not hearing Him at that exact moment. He may try to communicate with you during another part of the day. Pay attention to what happens in your life, to where He might be working to address the needs you have talked to Him about. Look for His working in conversations with others or situations that occur. Tune into physical or emotional reactions to interactions. He could be trying to tell you something. Listen in the quiet of night as you lie in bed on the edge of sleep.

During your time together with God, don't worry about evaluating what you are writing or experiencing. You can and should do that later. Below, you will find some guidelines on how to test your experience to validate that it is from God. But for now, allow yourself the freedom to listen expectantly for His voice. While we can't tell you exactly what it will be like, since God will deal uniquely with each person, we want to give you some ideas about what to look for. If you have trouble concentrating because other thoughts are distracting you—a list of groceries, things you need to get done that day, a relationship you feel anxious about—write those thoughts on your journal page. Tell God you feel distracted, that you need to talk about these concerns first; then, when you feel more settled, come back to the passages and questions. Take your time answering the questions. If it becomes too painful, take a break. Talk to a trusted friend for support.

> "Call to me and I will answer you and tell you great and unsearchable things you do not know."
> JEREMIAH 33:3

We have also included a small-group discussion guide at the end of each chapter. Although you will work through this material on your own, it can be even more powerful to share your experiences with others on the same journey. Our experience with women's small groups is that God's healing power is greatly increased when we boldly discuss our struggles, our discoveries, and the deepest longings of our heart with others. If you have the opportunity to gather a group of women you feel safe with, use this material as a launching pad for more meaningful sharing. However, even if you are doing this on your own, we encourage you to share some of the things God reveals to you with at least one other person—a spouse, a family member, a friend. Discussing His work in your life solidifies the truth He longs for you to take hold of. It makes your journey toward deeper relationship with Him more real and tangible.

In the "Experiences with God" section of each chapter we have included stories that women have shared with us about God's direct response to their needs. We hope that their experiences will encourage you with how intimate and relevant your Father longs to be with you.

Testing Your Experience

Here are some questions you can ask yourself about what you are hearing that will help validate your experience as trustworthy:

- Is it consistent with Scripture?
- Is it consistent with the character of God?
- Does it lead to change or growth in your life?
- Does it lead to the restoration of relationships?
- Is there a sense of healing, release from past sin or pain?
- Is there a sense of peace or calmness, a lessening of anxiety, a sense of contentment where once there was striving?
- Does it sound more like something you would say than something God would say?

◆ Does it lead to conviction instead of guilt? (On the following pages you will find further material to help you differentiate between conviction and guilt.)

There is a distinct difference between the conviction of the Holy Spirit and the condemnation of the devil, because the two speak different languages. The characteristics of each—listed in the chart on the following page—should help you distinguish whose voice you are hearing. However, we sometimes mistake Satan's voice for God's, because Satan's voice fits so well with our own distortions and misunderstandings about God and how we think He feels about us. But God speaks to us in a way that is completely different from the condemnation of Satan. You may need to review these descriptions again over the course of your journey through this workbook. Use these as a guideline when you are listening for God's voice. As you practice, it will become easier to distinguish the difference, and you will be able to clearly hear God's responses as you share your heart with Him.

The Bible is clear about the fact that God actively pursues a personal relationship with His children. He delights in you and desires to bring restoration to the painful places in your life. He offers Himself as a refuge from fear and anxiety. He holds out His strength to those who are weak, and He longs to mourn with those who are broken. He is here for you—anytime you come—He is here for you.

He is gently calling, "Come with Me."

Conviction of the Holy Spirit	Condemnation of the Evil One
Tone of voice: gentle, loving, imploring, beseeching, urging our return to Him.	**Tone of voice:** accusing, nagging, mocking voice. His voice generates fear, causes confusion and a sense of rejection.
Specific: tells you to take one specific action in response to sin. Freedom follows.	**Vague and general:** generates a blanketing sense of guilt, as though everything is wrong and there is no action you can take to overcome. Creates a sense of hopelessness and weakness.
Encouraging: says you can rely on His power, not your strength.	**Discouraging:** attacks your self-image, tells you that you are weak, that you are not special to God.
Releases you from the past: tells you your sin is forgiven, removed, never to be held against you.	**Throws your past in your face:** replays your sin and shame, reminds you of all your poor choices and bad decisions.
Attracts you to Him: generates an expectancy of kindness, love, forgiveness, a new beginning with His help. Speaks of your permanent relationship with Him.	**Rejecting:** produces the feeling that God has rejected you as unworthy and unholy, speaks of God as your judge and you as a miserable sinner.
Draws you into fellowship: sends others to minister to you in love. Speaks of His unchanging nature and His steadfast love, even when you fail Him.	**Isolates you:** gives suggestions that cause you to withdraw from others and to assume they will also reject you.
Tells the truth: states the facts about you and God.	**Focuses on negative feelings:** tells you the way you feel is the way things are; that the guilt, despair, hopelessness, the doubt about God's love for you are truth.

(Adapted from *World Christian* news bulletin, vol. 6, no. 2, February 1993)

God, I am afraid
Afraid to go where
　　you might lead me
Afraid to stay where
　　I've been so long

I am broken
I am tired
I am longing for your touch

Sweep through me
Gently woo me
Give me courage as I come

Journaling

Tell God what you are hoping for—what you want from Him—as you work through this material.

_____

_____

_____

_____

_____

_____

_____

_____

_____

_____

_____

_____

_____

_____

_____

_____

_____

_____

_____

_____

_____

_____

_____

Small-Group Discussion Questions

You are about to enter into a unique experience of wrestling with some of your feelings about your relationship with God. As you begin this journey, take some time to share with the group how you are feeling about entering this process.

- How would you describe your relationship with God right now?

- What do you think about the idea of God speaking to you specifically?

- What fears or concerns do you have about addressing these issues?

Journaling

Write to Him about any ways you feel differently about yourself or Him after working through this chapter.

_____

_____

_____

_____

_____

_____

_____

_____

_____

_____

_____

_____

_____

_____

_____

_____

_____

_____

_____

_____

_____

2

God Loves Us,
Not Our Performance

"I am in love with you just as you are."

Angela's Story

I was raised in a conservative Baptist community in the South. The whole culture taught that there is a perfect way to be a proper Christian young lady. I was always expected to perform at my best—to be spiritual, to be a good daughter, to follow the rules. There was no room to fail. If I was capable of doing something, I needed to do it and do it well. Being average was not acceptable. There was always someone there making sure I didn't fall outside the guidelines.

Today I'm still trying to do things perfectly, ensuring that everything is just right—that the tennis shoes are white, that the silverware is stacked in the drawer, that the anger doesn't go over the top, that I never roll my eyes in disgust, that I am on time no matter what, that I appear put together.

I have this perception that God expects perfection from me, too. I have to be perfect to be worthy of His love. I have to excel in everything I am capable of doing because being average is not good enough for God. When I am imperfect in my own eyes it's like I hear God saying, "Why didn't you get an A+ if you were capable of it?" I'm so afraid He is disappointed in me.

Most of us learned early on that our behavior could win or lose us love. When we were children, our parents, teachers, churches, and friends told us what they expected from us and then decided whether or not our behavior was acceptable. Many of us were often unable to please the very people we wanted to believe in us. And even as we grew older and realized that their expectations were unattainable, we continued to try, hoping that someday we could earn their love.

> "Sow for yourselves righteousness, reap the fruit of unfailing love, and break up your unplowed ground; for it is time to seek the LORD . . . you have eaten the fruit of deception. Because you have depended on your own strength and on your many warriors."
> HOSEA 10:12–13

Some of us are still trying to earn someone's acceptance, still attempting to prove to someone that we are worth loving. We struggle with guilt, shame, and self-contempt, joining with voices from the past, placing unreasonable expectations on ourselves. It's not enough to take care of our families and do well at our jobs. We also need to take care of our friends, have our devotions every morning, serve on three or four committees at church, be the team mom, exercise three times a week, and occasionally throw a fabulous gourmet soiree! We tell ourselves that if we try hard enough, we will finally become what we should be.

This pattern of thinking seeps into our relationship with God, re-creating Him into someone else we have to perform for—someone else who is more concerned with correct behavior than with an intimate relationship. Our spiritual life becomes all about what we do, leaving us fearful that we are a constant disappointment to Him. Forgiveness and acceptance seem like mere words, luxuries we are unable to experience. We long to feel embraced and encouraged, to give up all the striving, but it seems impossible that God might truly love us just as we are.

Journaling

Isaiah understood humanity's focus on performance. Explore the following passages, in which he writes to the Israelites whose distorted images of God made it difficult for them to accept His invitation to find rest and comfort.

> *Very well then, with foreign lips and strange tongues God will speak to this people, to whom he said, "This is the resting place, let the weary rest;" and "This is the place of repose"— but they would not listen. So then, the word of the LORD to them will become: Do and do, do and do, rule on rule, rule on rule; a little here, a little there—so that they will go and fall backward, be injured and snared and captured . . . "for we have made a lie our refuge and falsehood our hiding place." (ISAIAH 28:11–13, 15)*

> *This is what the Sovereign LORD, the Holy One of Israel says: "In repentance and rest is your salvation, in quietness and trust is your strength, but you would have none of it." (ISAIAH 30:15)*

Where are you weary in your life? Where are you striving, pushing yourself to frustration or exhaustion? Pour out your heart to Him about your intensity in these areas.

_____

_____

_____

_____

_____

_____

_____

_____

Are you more comfortable doing the right things, following the rules, than you are resting in His presence? Why?

_____

_____

_____

_____

_____

_____

_____

_____

Write about how it feels for you to be alone with God and rest. Explore what prevents you from feeling completely comfortable in His presence. What are you afraid God might be thinking about you? Speak to Him honestly about this.

_____

_____

_____

_____

_____

_____

_____

Where do these falsehoods or distortions come from that hold you back from resting in Him? Who might have taught you to think this way?

_____

_____

_____

_____

_____

_____

_____

_____

_____

"Repose" means the act of resting, freedom from anxiety, calmness, tranquility. It means "to lie supported by something." Describe what it would look like for you to rest in Him when you are weary.

_____

_____

_____

_____

_____

_____

Talk to God about any fears or hesitations you have about pursuing Him as your resting place, your place of repose. Ask God to speak to you about what He wants for you regarding these areas of striving in your life. Over the next week, write what you hear or see or feel related to this.

_____

_____

_____

_____

_____

_____

_____

_____

～ Debra's Story ～

My family was impossible to please. My grandmothers were constantly critical. They both had huge expectations of me. They were definite about what I should do with my life. When I didn't do things the way they wanted me to, I was a failure in their eyes. They'd say, "You're really blowing it. You're turning out just like your mother." My parents were the same. They never gave strokes for anything, never validated my achievements. The things I accomplished were either not done as well as they should have been or were not significant enough to be recognized.

My religious training in Catholic school led me to believe that God is just like that. The nuns always told me I didn't measure up. I looked up to them, and they made me feel awful, like a guilty person always needing to go to confession. Even now, after years of being a Christian, I'm sure God is shaking His head and wondering when I am going to shape up. I keep trying to find a way to earn His love and acceptance. I've done tons of ministry, tons of quiet time materials and Bible studies. I try to live without sin, but I never feel like it's enough. I'm constantly setting goals and trying to do it right, but I'm always feeling like a failure. ～

Journaling

Some of us live by the lie that we're never good enough, that we can never make up for the sins we've committed, that we'll never measure up. As you read these passages, allow yourself to begin to hear God express His desire to deal with your failures and inadequacies with compassion and forgiveness. There is acceptance waiting for you!

> *The LORD is compassionate and gracious, slow to anger, abounding in love. He will not always accuse, nor will he harbor his anger forever; he does not treat us as our sins deserve or repay us according to our iniquities.* (PSALM 103:8–10)

> *Praise the LORD, O my soul, and forget not all his benefits— who forgives all your sins and heals all your diseases, who redeems your life from the pit and crowns you with love and compassion, who satisfies your desires with good things so that your youth is renewed like the eagle's.* (PSALM 103:2–5)

Are you waiting for God to punish you for something in your past or present? A sin or mistake that you will eventually have to pay for? Is it possible you are waiting for Him to pull the rug out from under you? Explore this.

_____

_____

_____

_____

_____

_____

_____

_____

_____

> "For the Lord your God is a merciful God, He will not fail you, or destroy you."
> DEUTERONOMY 4:31
> (Amplified Version)

Write about how you feel accused or unforgivable because of this issue. Tell Him the whole story—how this event/situation happened, how you feel about what you've done or what you're still doing. Tell Him about your fears and anxieties. Tell Him if you are afraid that He cannot or will not forgive you.

_____

_____

_____

_____

_____

_____

_____

_____

_____

_____

_____

_____

_____

_____

_____

Ask Him to speak to you about how He feels about you and how He wants to renew you.

_____

_____

_____

_____

_____

_____

_____

_____

_____

_____

_____

_____

Our friend Sharla Jackson shared this song with us. She told us, "I wrote 'Forgiven' for a friend who just couldn't grasp God's grace and felt it applied to everyone but herself. I later thought maybe I wrote the song for ME!" Maybe she wrote it for you, too.

Forgiven
If you could see yourself through my eyes
If you could step inside my heart and realize
The beauty that I see and generosity
So strong, compassionate and wise

Let it all go, you're forgiven
Let Him heal those wounds that are so deep
Crawl upon His lap and feel His arms wrap around you
Release it, and lay it at His feet

If you could see yourself through His eyes
If you could separate the truth from lies
He sees a precious soul, and He longs to make you whole
He loves you, and He hears your desperate cries

For He knows the plans He has for you
Not for evil, but for good
To give you a future and a hope
You've been covered with His blood

So let it all go, you're forgiven
Let Him heal those wounds that are so deep
Crawl upon His lap and feel His arms wrap around you
Release it, and lay it at His feet
You're forgiven

"I am in love with you just as you are." 49

Journaling

Our internal voice can often be extremely negative, condemning us at every opportunity. The Evil One works against us, creating damaging thinking patterns. These voices can get so loud that we lose the ability to hear God's voice or to function in relationships the way we would like to. Try to put aside those all too familiar voices as you work through these passages and listen for something new. Listen for God's gentle, accepting voice, expressing His longing to give you peacefulness in those areas where you experience constant condemnation.

This then is how we know that we belong to the truth, and how we set our hearts at rest in his presence whenever our hearts condemn us. For God is greater than our hearts, and he knows everything. (1 John 3:19–20)

What do the loud, condemning voices in your head sound like? What do they say? What failures or inadequacies do they focus on?

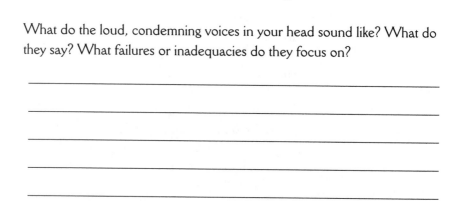

_____

_____

_____

_____

_____

_____

_____

_____

_____

_____

We are good at condemning ourselves. But we also often pass on that condemnation to others. We accuse others of being failures in the very areas in which we are so afraid of failing. Who might you be passing your condemnation on to? Write about how you see yourself doing this—what behavior or situations trigger your condemnation? If you are not sure of how or where you might be doing this, ask God to make you aware of any such patterns in your life. You could also ask people in your life to identify what you are critical about. (Extra points to you if you attempt this difficult step!)

> "My grace is sufficient for you, for my power is made perfect in weakness."
> 2 CORINTHIANS 12:9

_____

_____

_____

_____

_____

_____

_____

_____

_____

What are you afraid will happen if you do not communicate your disapproval of their behavior?

_____

_____

_____

_____

_____

_____

_____

_____

Ask God to talk to you about how you could begin to release others from your condemnation and "set their hearts at rest." Ask God what He will do to help you let go of this pattern.

_____

_____

_____

_____

_____

_____

_____

_____

For I am convinced that neither death nor life, neither angels nor demons, neither the present nor the future, nor any powers, neither height nor depth, nor anything else in all creation, will be able to separate us from the love of God that is in Christ Jesus our Lord. (ROMANS 8:38)

Even with his history as a violent persecutor of Christians, the apostle Paul was sure of God's love for him. What would it take to convince you of this in your life? Talk to God about your need to be convinced in a personal way of His strong, accepting love for you.

_____

_____

_____

_____

_____

_____

_____

_____

_____

_____

_____

_____

_____

Experiences with God

I (Kathy) relate to this chapter the most and have experienced a new relationship with God over the course of these past few years. Here is a glimpse of my own journey to encourage you with how relevant God wants to be in every area of our lives.

In my life it seems I have always felt the need to do more. To perform better, to achieve the best, to make sure I looked good in the eyes of others. I knew deep in my heart that people's perceptions of me and the truth of how I felt inside were very different. Yet I truly did not know what to do with those feelings. On the outside, I appeared together, strong, organized, overly capable. Inside, I felt lonely, detached, tormented by voices in my head that always told me what I did wasn't good enough.

I never made the connection between how I lived my life and my family history until I became part of a women's small group and started talking more freely about my past. As I made myself more vulnerable (very hard for me to do because I was so used to being in control and together), the wounds of my past began to open. I began to see, for the first time, how the brokenness in my family had affected me. As an adult, I started to realize how I had taken care of others since I was very young, but that no one really took care of me. Looking at this reality hurt me deeply. As I opened up to these women and shared my painful memories with them, they helped me make connections between my relationship with my family and others and how I had transferred this brokenness into my relationship with God. They asked me questions like, "Whose voice are you hearing in this moment? How else was this negative message communicated to you? Which of these voices have you put into God's mouth?" The connections were hard to look at, and I was torn between my desire to close this Pandora's box I had opened and the need to keep going through the process in search of God's healing.

Jesus' statement that "The truth will set you free" (John 8:32) became real to me. As I began to communicate with my family members and others more openly, I tasted a bit of the freedom that comes from truth. I discussed with my husband, for the first time, sins from my past that I had kept under lock and key. Truth began to prevail in my life rather than lies and pretenses. God opened the doors by providing these women to share with. Over a period of time He gently led me to see through His eyes who I was, to more clearly identify why I struggled with certain feelings of insecurity and low self-esteem.

Over the past few years, I have experienced Him in many ways. Sometimes a friend will share a struggle, and it will directly tap into one of my painful experiences, and He will lead me to look more clearly at that wound. Other times, a Scripture will jump out at me from every angle, and I can see Him prompting me to explore its meaning in my life. Recently I was in church (not paying attention to the message!) flipping through the pages of my Bible. Clearly before me was Hosea 10:13, and the words struck me deeply: "You have eaten the fruit of deception. . . . you have depended on your own strength and on your many warriors." God knew I had been struggling with weariness and exhaustion, and I am certain that He

"I am in love with you just as you are."   55

directed me to those verses in that moment. I believe He wanted me to connect with the deception of depending on my own strength, thinking I have to fight all my battles alone. He knew in that moment, in the midst of the church service, that this was the truth I needed to hear. I didn't feel completely changed just from reading that one verse, but over the course of the next few days, almost everything I read or heard was related to resting in His arms and allowing Him to be my strength. And I began to get the message.

Sometimes His voice has beckoned in the middle of the night—in the midst of a struggle—and I have heard Him reveal a truth He wants me to grasp about His true character or who I am in His eyes. One night I was lying alone in the dark, feeling guilty about the many blessings in my life when inside I was horridly ashamed of past sin. I kept saying to myself, *When is God going to stop tormenting me with blessings! I deserve punishment for my sins, and I never seem to get any relief, only more good things!* Then I heard His voice somewhere inside me speak strongly and clearly, yet ever so gently. *Kathy, when are you going to see that this is not who I am? When are you going to embrace all that I have for your life, to rest in it, to receive My good gifts?* I knew it was God because I was overwhelmed by the truth and power of His words. They left an indelible mark on my heart. To this day, I can remember that night. It's something to grasp on to when I begin to travel down the shame road again. I've discovered an entirely new kind of relationship with Him—deeper and more real than I ever expected.

Heidi's Experience

I had been struggling in my walk with the Lord. For a long time I had pictured Him as an aloof, distant dictator who is most interested in my performance. When I don't *do,* I don't feel worthy of God's love and acceptance. This view of Him keeps me from wanting to spend time with Him in prayer because I constantly am ashamed of my performance, as if I am not measuring up to His expectations and He is sitting high on His throne waiting for me to get my act together. I carry a perpetual sense of shame that I continually disappoint Him, and I struggle with never feeling good enough in almost every aspect of my life. Recently, however, I had an experience with God that finally broke down some of these walls.

One afternoon as my young daughter was napping, my heart became heavily burdened for several close friends who were going through major trials in their lives. As I thought about their struggles, I felt an overwhelming doubt that the Lord was in control. Instead, I felt that He was expecting *me* to do something. The more I dwelt on this, the more anxious I became. Because these people live far from me, I felt my hands were tied. I couldn't do anything for them but pray. And somehow praying didn't feel like enough. Once again, I was not living up to His expectations.

Despite my usual pattern of resisting being with the Lord, the burden this particular afternoon was too much for me to bear alone. I knew I had to share some of my overwhelming feelings with Him. I didn't really pray at first. Instead I looked up the word *sovereignty* in my Bible's concordance. Among the verses listed was Job 38:1–42:6. In this passage Job questions the Lord's sovereignty and the Lord replies with questions that Job can't possibly answer, reaffirming to Job that God is still in control of his life. I needed that same reassurance.

As I reflected on this passage, I felt His Holy Spirit in a way I have never experienced before. As I began to pray, my tense muscles started to relax. My clenched fists unfolded, and I began to breathe more calmly and evenly. I felt an overwhelming sense of safety, as if the Lord was physically embracing me through my spirit, calming my fear of His disapproval. I didn't feel ashamed or self-protective; instead I felt welcomed, invited. I was connected to the moment, totally there, washed over with warmth. I felt His Spirit gently say, *It's okay, Heidi—you don't have to carry this alone. Release it all to Me. Release yourself to My hands. I want you to share your burdens with Me—all that is heavy on your heart. Yes, I am the sovereign God of this world, but I am also the God who is interested in the intimate struggles of your life. I want you to crawl into your Daddy's lap. I want to be close to you. I want to comfort you.* This love and acceptance was not what I expected, but it was so powerful. It drew me in, making me want to stay in this place, experience more of this peace. Usually when I insist on being self-reliant, I feel cold, alone, and eventually in despair. Yet as I continued to pray, the Lord's compassion melted the cold and loneliness, making me feel warm, accepted, and at home.

Sitting on the floor by my bed, I found His acceptance overwhelming me and I began to sob as I poured out my anxieties to Him. I unleashed my heavy heart. I didn't just pray for the people who needed His help; I also repented of *my* faithlessness and all my doubts. I confessed my lack of trust and my feelings of inadequacy in my relationship with Him. As I wept He assured me of my true identity as His daughter, the daughter of a king.

My eyes were still closed, and I saw an image in my mind. It was a distinct, brilliant picture. I saw myself standing before God's throne, clothed in a white robe of royalty. I felt comfortable in this garment, like it was made exactly for me. I wasn't ashamed or uncomfortable. His eyes were gentle, and He was nothing like the dictator I have often expected Him to be. His eyes said I was completely adequate and whole, not a constant disappointment to Him. I felt peaceful. Overwhelmed with love. Sure of who I was.

After I finished praying, I felt different . . . lighter. My shoulders were weightless. What started out as a struggle turned out to be one of the most amazing times I have ever had with God. I was refreshed emotionally and spiritually, like never before.

"And I pray that you, being rooted and established in love, may have power, together with all the saints, to grasp how wide and long and high and deep is the love of Christ, and to know this love that surpasses knowledge."
EPHESIANS 3:17–19

Peg's Experience

For twenty years I have struggled with Crohn's disease, which is a chronic inflammation of the small intestine. I have severe episodes of cramps that come on suddenly and knock me off my feet for a few days at a time. This past fall I became so ill I ended up in the hospital. When intravenous drugs did not quiet my disease, surgery became necessary.

During my hospital stay God showed Himself to me in a personal, powerful way. Two days after surgery I had gotten out of bed into a chair. Movement was a great effort, but I knew it would help me heal. As I gripped the arms of the chair I felt like I was ninety-five years old, frail and sick. Although I was thin to begin with, I had lost twenty pounds in two weeks. I had numerous tubes that were extremely uncomfortable. My skin was cracked and marked from all the needles. I could only sponge bathe and was unable to wash my hair. I felt so poorly that I did not think I would get well. I thought, *This is my life, this is the rest of my life, right here in this hospital room.*

At that moment Julie, the nurse's assistant for the day, cheerfully swept into my room. I watched her as she began to change the sheets on my bed. Pretty, young, energetic, she reminded me of *me* before I got sick. Suddenly, sitting there in that chair, I felt stripped of everything. My health had been taken away. My life as I knew it, with all my groups and Bible studies and activities, had been taken away. I could do nothing. Even my kids, whom I hadn't seen in days, were being cared for by others. The most basic things—eating, drinking, moisturizing my skin, putting in contacts—weren't even an option at this point. Julie represented to me all that I had lost.

Overcome with shame at the condition I was in, I told the young nurse's assistant to go look at the picture on my window ledge of me in my women's group, taken earlier in the year. I wanted to make sure she knew I was more than the broken woman in front of her. "That is what I *really* look like," I said. As if that would matter! As if what I really looked like gave me value and worth and dignity! Humiliated, I was basing my value as a person on what I could do (nothing), what I looked like (sickly), what I could say (very little).

There are lots of negative reactions Julie could have had, but she did not patronize me, or feel sorry for me, or laugh at me, or think me pathetic. Instead she responded in respectful silence, continuing to straighten my room. Throughout the day she served me with great compassion, encouraging me to rest, speaking kind words, and doing for me all that I could not do for myself because my body was so weak. Julie's gentle demeanor did not demand a response. As a result, I was able to let go of my striving to prove my worth in her eyes, allowing myself to rest and receive her care.

As the days passed, the Lord began to restore my hope. I began to see progress in my recovery from surgery. I admitted my fears to Him and began to try to trust Him with the rest of my life, whether healthy or not. I had discovered that Julie was a sister in the Lord. As I thought of her I began to realize that all the words she'd spoken through her actions and attitudes were *His* words for me. I am His child, His precious child, dearly loved. Even at my lowest moments—especially at my lowest moments—when I have nothing left to offer or give, I am dearly loved.

> As you finish this chapter, reflect on how God loves you, not what you do.

Small-Group Discussion Questions

Use your time together to truthfully discuss the tendency to **do** in your lives. It's hard to talk about this, and it may be the first time you've said out loud that you struggle with feeling acceptable to God. These feelings are not sin. Sharing them can be a first step to changing them.

- What are the expectations from God or others you feel you need to live up to?

- Share with the group how you usually respond to these expectations.

- What if you stopped or slowed down? What would that mean about who you are?

Journaling

Write to Him about any ways you feel differently about yourself or Him after working through this chapter.

_____

_____

_____

_____

_____

_____

_____

_____

_____

_____

_____

_____

_____

_____

_____

_____

_____

_____

_____

_____

_____

GOD LOVES US, NOT OUR PERFORMANCE

3

God Wants to Connect
Intimately with Us

"I desire to be deeply intimate with you."

Jane's Story

I was twelve years old when my dad left and took my brothers with him. My mom went to work, and I was all alone. Suddenly I felt like I wasn't a part of anything bigger than myself. I often wondered why my parents didn't care enough about me to make their marriage work. What was wrong with me? Why wasn't I good enough to stay for? I worried that I had contributed to the break-up. If I had been a better child, maybe they would have stayed around. That time in my life taught me not to trust anyone, that I would always be left. I still miss my dad and wish he were more a part of my life, but he rarely calls me.

Now I always worry about being excluded by others. I'm paranoid about being left out. Even though I have a lot of relationships, I'm afraid that people are with me only because they have to be or because they feel sorry for me. Even in my marriage, I've been plagued by this belief that I'm not good enough for the relationship. I've been testing it from the beginning; sometimes consciously, sometimes unconsciously. I hear myself telling my husband that I'm not right for him, that I don't deserve him. Sometimes I'll say something inappropriate or unkind and then say, "See, you deserve someone better than me." I was sure that at some point I would do something that would cause him to reject me. I even became involved in an affair at one point. When I look back at that now, I can see that I was trying to ruin this good thing that God has given me. It was too scary waiting for my husband to *eventually reject me, so I tried to bring on the inevitable. But he's stayed with me, forcing me to believe in his love for me.*

I still have a hard time accepting that God wants to be personal and intimate with me. I can believe that He loves me because I'm His child and that He needs me to participate in building His kingdom, but He feels very far off. I struggle with believing that He wants to include me in an intimate relationship.

Journaling

Often we struggle with a personal and intimate relationship with God because we have not been singled out by someone who has treasured us. Rather, we may have been overlooked or even tossed aside by someone we thought would be there for us. Those painful experiences make it hard to believe that we could be valuable to anyone, even God. Knowing that He is different doesn't change the fact that it can feel terrifying to abandon ourselves to Him. We would rather protect ourselves from longing for Him and stay in control. The idea that God is intensely interested in us and desires a real and intimate connection with us seems like a fairy tale. But it's true! He is in continual pursuit of us. Not just other people—those who are better than us or more spiritual—but us! He is undaunted by our humanness, our sin, our failures. To Him, we are delightful!

For you are a people holy to the LORD your God. Out of all the peoples on the face of the earth, the LORD has chosen you to be his treasured possession. (DEUTERONOMY 14:2)

Who are the people in your life who failed to treasure you in the way you have longed to be treasured? Talk to God about the pain of this.

_____

_____

_____

_____

_____

_____

_____

_____

"On that day you will realize that I am in my Father, and you are in me, and I am in you. . . . He who loves me will be loved by my Father, and I too will love him and show myself to him."

JOHN 14:20–21

How do you respond emotionally to the idea that you are God's treasured possession? What happens inside you when you think about being that to Him?

_____

_____

_____

_____

_____

_____

_____

"I desire to be deeply intimate with you."   69

How would your life look different if you could really believe that you are a treasured possession of God?

_____

_____

_____

_____

_____

_____

Take some time to sit still and listen to God tell you how "[He] has chosen you to be his treasured possession." Write down anything you hear, see, or sense.

_____

_____

_____

_____

_____

_____

> *But Zion said, "The LORD has forsaken me, the LORD has forgotten me." "Can a mother forget the baby at her breast and have no compassion on the child she has borne? Though she may forget, I will not forget you! See, I have you engraved on the palms of my hands."* (ISAIAH 49:14–16)

Write about times in your life when you have felt forgotten or forsaken by God.

_____

_____

_____

_____

_____

Now ask Him to bring to mind ways in which He was there in those moments you felt forsaken.

_____

_____

_____

_____

_____

Tell God what it feels like to be "engraved on the palms of [His] hands" (e.g., comforting, scary, unsettling, exciting).

_____

_____

_____

_____

_____

⟿ Leslie's Story ⟿

Most of my childhood I was molested by my older brother. Even though he was abusive to me, I adored him. He gave me special attention and protected me from other kids. I thought that he really loved me. But when I eventually refused to let him touch me anymore, he totally rejected me. He had controlled our whole relationship and had always been able to get what he wanted. When he could no longer do that, he wanted nothing to do with me. I decided then that I would never be at the mercy of anyone else. I became determined to control relationships so I would be safe. Everyone I chose to be involved with was submissive. I picked weak boyfriends who would let me control them. I needed to feel I was the one who had the power in the relationship.

When I'm not in a one-up position, I feel anxious about being rejected. I am even afraid to give up control to God. I'm afraid He'll let something bad happen. I don't think that He wants bad things to happen to me. I just don't believe He'll make sure they don't. If I'm in control, I feel like I have a better chance of making sure things go the way I want. I'm too afraid to rely on God for my well-being. ⟿

Journaling

We work so hard at making our world predictable and logical. We move away from our hearts and into our heads because it is safer there. We put God into a little box and decide how big we will let Him be. We decide how He will or won't work, what He does or doesn't think about us. We have it all figured out. But in quiet moments we know something is wrong. We yearn for more. Our hearts are homesick for the Father.

O God, you are my God, earnestly I seek you; my soul thirsts for you, my body longs for you, in a dry and weary land where there is no water. (PSALM 63:1)

I spread out my hands to you; my soul thirsts for you like a parched land. (PSALM 143:6)

As the deer pants for streams of water, so my soul pants for you, O God. My soul thirsts for God, for the living God. When can I go and meet with God? My tears have been my food day and night. (PSALM 42:1–3)

In your life, what usually creates separation or distance between you and God?

_____

_____

_____

_____

"I desire to be deeply intimate with you." 73

_____

_____

What re-creates a thirst for Him? Is it crisis, anxiety, loneliness?

_____

_____

_____

_____

_____

> "Come to me, all you who are weary and burdened, and I will give you rest. Take my yoke upon you and learn from me, for I am gentle and humble in heart, and you will find rest for your souls."
>
> MATTHEW 11:28–29

What are you thirsting for from Him?

_____

_____

_____

_____

This is what the Lord *Almighty says: "I am very jealous for Zion; I am burning with jealousy for her." (ZECHARIAH 8:2)*

What feeling does being sought after like this stir up in you? Share these feelings with God. Talk to Him about what it feels like to be the object of His jealousy.

_____

_____

_____

_____

_____

_____

Why is it hard to imagine that God would be jealous for you?

_____

_____

_____

_____

_____

Now ask Him to show you why He is jealous for you. Listen to His voice. Filter out all the messages about how He couldn't possibly feel that intensely about you and allow His Spirit to speak to you about His deep love for you. What are you experiencing as you sit still?

_____

_____

_____

_____

_____

_____

_____

Experiences with God

Sonia's Experience

I was reading this passage one day.

> *A large crowd followed and pressed around him. And a woman was there who had been subject to bleeding for twelve years. She had suffered a great deal under the care of many doctors and had spent all she had, yet instead of getting better she grew worse. When she heard about Jesus, she came up behind him in the crowd and touched his cloak, because she thought, "If I just touch his clothes, I will be healed." Immediately her bleeding stopped and she felt in her body that she was freed from her suffering.*
>
> *At once Jesus realized that power had gone out from him. He turned around in the crowd and asked, "Who touched my clothes?"*
>
> *"You see the people crowding against you," his disciples answered, "and yet you can ask, 'Who touched me?'"*
>
> *But Jesus kept looking around to see who had done it. Then the woman, knowing what had happened to her, came and fell at his feet and, trembling with fear, told him the whole truth. He said to her, "Daughter, your faith has healed you. Go in peace and be freed from your suffering."* (MARK 5:24–34)

I had read the story many times before, but for some reason, that day, I found myself stuck on something I'd never paid attention to before. I found myself wondering why it was so important for Jesus to find the woman who had touched Him. Surely He knew what had happened. Someone had been healed. Someone who believed He had the power to restore her had reached out to touch Him. Why was it so important that He find her and talk to her? Didn't He already know who she was? It wasn't that He wanted to confront her about some sin or take the healing from her, because He didn't do that. I found myself wondering if perhaps it was because He wanted to give her something more. Maybe He wanted to give her permission to enjoy her healing, to affirm it, to look her in the face and tell her it was okay, that what she thought she had taken from Him was something He desired to freely give her.

Suddenly the story felt very personal. Like I was the woman, trembling with fear, afraid to look Him in the eye, afraid He would be displeased with me. Somewhere deep inside I heard God say, "You always underestimate how intimate and personal I want to be with you." He's right. I don't expect Him to move into my life to bring change or healing. I think I am a bother when I come to Him with my needs. I think of my pain as something I need to handle. I think of myself as just a face in the crowd. But I am wrong. He told me that day that He wants to meet me individually, He wants to free

> "My sheep listen to my voice; I know them, and they follow me. I give them eternal life, and they shall never perish; no one can snatch them out of my hand."
> JOHN 10:27–28

me from my suffering, He wants to look me in the face and call me "daughter," too.

Caroline's Experience

Today I saw God's eyes. I saw God's heart. The experience touched me deeply. I was at a church retreat and spoke with Dan, a man whose daughter was struggling with some major issues in her life. As he spoke about his hope for her healing, I saw a side of a daddy I had not seen before. He was heartbroken, *not by her but for her.* He was distraught, not because of her behavior but because she was so ashamed of her situation. He repeatedly said, "I just don't want her to be stuck in shame."

When I looked into Dan's tear-filled eyes as he spoke about his daughter, I saw a picture of Jesus. It touched me to my core. I saw a daddy who loved his daughter with an intense, deep love and was devastated that she was hurting. I saw a father who longed for his daughter to be free of shame. I saw a father who wept over his daughter's brokenness. It gave me a tangible image, a powerful glimpse of God, my Father, who cares this deeply for me—who cares even more. Because I don't have an earthly father who feels that way, I sometimes have difficulty imagining God as that kind of father.

I didn't realize the intensity of my feelings as we were having the conversation. It was when I got into the car afterward and shared the interaction with my husband that I realized its depth. As

I described the look in Dan's eyes, I was overcome with emotion. And I know when I am overwhelmed like this that God is telling me to hear Him in it. As I looked at the intense, amazing feelings Dan had for his daughter, I was left with the strong impression that this is what God feels for me. He showed me that day that He is my Abba, my Daddy, the one who feels my pain, who knows my heart. How I have longed to have a daddy to love me this deeply! And indeed I do!

As you finish this chapter, reflect on how God desires to intimately connect with you.

Small-Group Discussion Questions

- ✆ Share your journaling about times in your life when you have felt forgotten or forsaken by God (see pg. 71).

- ✆ How do you protect yourself from being vulnerable now?

- ✆ In this chapter you've been exploring what it means to be treasured by God. Share ways you long for Him to demonstrate this in your life and ways He is already doing this.

Journaling

Write to Him about any ways you feel differently about yourself or Him after working through this chapter.

_____

_____

_____

_____

_____

_____

_____

_____

_____

_____

_____

_____

_____

_____

_____

_____

_____

_____

4

God Is Working on Our Behalf

"I long to rescue and restore you."

Corrine's Story

I've been on my own since I was little. My brothers and I got very little help or encouragement from my parents. As long as we were busy, that's all they cared about, so I learned to take care of myself. Now I don't want to be a burden to anyone. When people offer to help me with something, I usually say no because I don't want to bother them. I don't expect anyone to take care of me. I'm the only one I can count on. But I notice that I get angry and resentful because there's no one there to nurture me. I give and give with little recognition or appreciation. People just expect me to take care of things.

I feel this anger a lot in my marriage. I married someone who doesn't pay much attention to me. I feel like I'm always thinking about how I can make his life easier, but he rarely thinks about my needs. He sends me the same message that my parents did—that I'm on my own.

In my relationship with God I have that same feeling. I think He wants me to take care of things myself. I know He loves me, but I don't think of Him as interested in the details of my life. He is there for me, but I don't want to be a burden or a bother to Him. If I ask for something, He will probably answer, but I don't think He wants to be that involved. I don't expect Him to take care of me. If I have desires that I want to be fulfilled, it's my job to make them happen. My happiness in life is up to me. ∾

Journaling

Do you relate to that sense of being on your own, wondering if God is really there for you? Does He seem distant and unconcerned with your struggles? Maybe you've had to handle life on your own for so long that you have no idea what it would be like to get some help. You pray, and yet nothing seems to change—you're stuck with the same situation, the same pain, and the same feeling of having to deal with life on your own.

Many of us struggle with the fear that God is unconcerned or uninvolved with our needs. We feel alone and helpless, wondering where in the world He is when we need Him most. So we give up looking for His involvement. We find ways to take care of ourselves or go without. We've learned not to expect too much from others and to protect ourselves from becoming too dependent on anyone, so we withhold from God, too, afraid that if we become too vulnerable with Him we will be left hanging or made a fool of.

"Listen to me . . . you whom I have upheld since you were conceived, and have carried since your birth. Even to your old age and gray hairs I am he, I am he who will sustain you. I have made you and I will carry you; I will sustain you and I will rescue you." (ISAIAH 46:3–4)

As you look back over your experiences, where does it seem as if God did not sustain or carry, where He did not rescue? Talk to God about this. Write to Him about your anger, your hurt, whatever your feelings are. Tell Him what you needed from Him.

_____

_____

_____

_____

_____

_____

_____

_____

_____

_____

Ask God to talk to you about where He was during those moments in your life. Ask Him to bring to mind ways in which He was there in the painful moments—perhaps through someone else or through preventing further or more severe damage.

_____

_____

_____

_____

_____

_____

_____

_____

_____

_____

_____

_____

Write about times when He did rescue and sustain. Write about all the rescues you can think of.

_____

_____

_____

_____

_____

_____

_____

_____

_____

_____

_____

_____

Holly's Story

Appearances were everything in my family. The house, the car, the clothes—everything had to be just so. There was a big focus on physical appearance. The outfit had to be perfect or it was not good enough. I needed to have the matching socks, shoes, and hair accessories—from head to foot, my wardrobe had to be just right. And to make the package complete, I was supposed to be perfect—academically, socially, and spiritually. My mother believed that's how you get love. I learned to believe that, too. Outside I looked so together, but inside I had such emptiness. My mother gave me lots of material things but withheld what I really needed.

My parents had divorced by the time I was seven, and my father withdrew from me emotionally. There was no way to fill up the hole inside. By the time I was in eighth grade I was using drugs to cope. I remember going to school one day totally high and everyone knew it. I got in big trouble. I freaked out and had a panic attack. My mom didn't know what to do with me. She made attempts to get me some help, but I remember that when I came back to school I had a brand-new outfit. That was her way of fixing things. She did a lot of shopping after a crisis. She would say, "We need to fix that." Then she would buy a lot of stuff to make it right.

The emptiness is still there. So I shop and eat to fill it. When I don't have enough money to buy all the pieces to an outfit for the kids or for me, I feel shame. Then I use food to comfort myself. Food is so tangible and available. I keep using it because I don't have as much of the other stuff I want in my life.

I don't feel like I have what I need from God either. I'm afraid to go to Him until I get everything just right. Then I expect Him to withhold help from me or to bless somebody else rather than me because I haven't done well enough. My reaction is to withhold myself from Him to avoid feeling disappointed when He doesn't nurture me. I don't trust Him to give me what I need, so I have to get it for myself.

Journaling

The engulfing waters threatened me, the deep surrounded me; seaweed was wrapped around my head. To the roots of the mountains I sank down; the earth beneath barred me in forever. But you brought my life up from the pit, O LORD my God. (JONAH 2:5–6)

I waited patiently for the LORD; he turned to me and heard my cry. He lifted me out of the slimy pit, out of the mud and mire; he set my feet on a rock and gave me a firm place to stand. He put a new song in my mouth, a hymn of praise to our

God. Many will see and fear and put their trust in the LORD.
(PSALM 40:1–3)

Tell God the cry of your heart. Write to Him about the frustration of your slimy pit. Tell Him about any fears you may have about not being rescued from feelings or behaviors you feel stuck in.

_____

_____

_____

_____

_____

What might it look like to have a "firm place to stand"? How might your thinking, your behavior, be different?

_____

_____

_____

_____

_____

"I have loved you
with an everlasting love;
I have drawn you with
loving-kindness. I will build
you up again and you
will be rebuilt."
JEREMIAH 31:3–4

Look back at the rescues you wrote about on page 86. Choose one or two and write a song or letter of praise to God for this.

_____

_____

_____

_____

What if God doesn't get tired of you? What if He is eager to help? Not just other people, but you! What if your need for strength to deal with your kids, or wisdom to handle a conflict with your spouse, or nurture to carry you through a crisis . . . what if all that help is available? What if He is tangibly there in the middle of all your regular, stressful days?

Do you not know? Have you not heard? The LORD is the everlasting God, the Creator of the ends of the earth. He will not grow tired or weary, and his understanding no one can fathom. He gives strength to the weary and increases the power of the weak. Even youths grow tired and weary, and young men stumble and fall; but those who hope in the LORD will renew their strength. They will soar on wings like eagles; they will run and not grow weary, they will walk and not be faint. (ISAIAH 40:28–31)

Where is there a sense of weariness in you? What is it that you are tired of? What makes it hard to hang onto hope?

_____

_____

_____

_____

_____

Are you afraid that God grows weary of your struggles? Are you afraid He is tired of you needing His help in this area? Talk to Him about your fears.

_____

_____

_____

_____

_____

Ask God to talk to you about how He feels about this need in you, about your helplessness in this area.

_____

_____

_____

_____

Ask God to help you imagine soaring above those things that cause you to stumble. Write about what you are picturing. Ask Him to help you identify a next step to take to pursue soaring.

_____

_____

_____

_____

_____

"I will restore you to health and heal your wounds."

(JEREMIAH 30:17)

See! The winter is past; the rains are over and gone. Flowers appear on the earth; the season of singing has come.

(SONG OF SOLOMON 2:11–12)

Write about any wounds you are aware of in your significant relationships and any ideas God brings to mind about how you might begin restoring those relationships.

_____

_____

_____

_____

_____

What might it look like if God brought a "season of singing" into these areas or relationships?

_____

_____

_____

_____

_____

Talk to God about bringing more "singing" into your life. Tell Him where you need Him to work and what kind of healing you desire there. Ask Him to teach you about His nurturing heart. What are you sensing as you sit still with Him?

_____

_____

_____

_____

"The LORD your God is with you, he is mighty to save. He will take great delight in you, he will quiet you with his love, he will rejoice over you with singing."
ZEPHANIAH 3:17

Experiences with God

Kara's Experience

I woke up this morning mad. I am mad at God. I know in my head that He is a God who rescues, that He desires for me to rest in Him, to give up my control and let Him carry and sustain me. I know all this, but somehow I feel on my own, left with having to get the dirty work of life done. I'm the one who has to get up and take care of my family, meet the needs of my friends, go without. I sound like a spoiled brat, but this is truly how I feel. I pray for help and sense Him saying, *Rest, Kara. I will take care of you. I will see you through your day*, but I resist. I'm like a dog fighting against being leashed, pulling against my master's hand.

Then a friend shared an amazing story with me, and I saw an image of myself. She saw a father on a bicycle grinding up a difficult hill in our neighborhood. Behind him was his young daughter on her bike. There was a rope between them, and he was pulling her up the hill. The little girl was pedaling as fast as she could, thinking she was doing all the work. But the rope between them was taut. The reality was that her daddy was pulling her up the hill. All her expended energy and furious pedaling was unnecessary.

This little girl is me! I think I have to do it all by myself. I pedal like a maniac, pumping until I'm exhausted, thinking I alone have to power myself up to the top of the hill. But the truth is that I am on a lead rope. Why can't I relax and let Him pull me, knowing His strength is enough?

I think it's because I have always been in control. I've always had to be. Or at least I thought I had to be. I'm learning that I don't need to anymore. I have a Father who's got me on a lead line. He's pulling me up the hill, exerting His energy on my behalf, and maybe I can stop pedaling so furiously.

"Do not be afraid or discouraged because of this vast army. For the battle is not yours, but God's. . . . You will not have to fight this battle. Take up your positions; stand firm and see the deliverance the LORD will give you." 2 CHRONICLES 20:15, 17

Wanda's Experience

I was lying in bed in the dark one night, struggling with all that was going on in my life. There was so much turmoil. My work situation was extremely stressful. I felt harassed and abused there but afraid to leave. I had a lump the doctor thought might be cancerous, and I had had cancer once before. Some close friends I had trusted were betraying me. Amidst all of this, I was feeling very distant from God. I was struggling with trust and peace, afraid that He wouldn't help—not because He doesn't care but because He thinks all the trouble will make me stronger. In my mind, being miserable equals spiritual maturity!

I had never gone to God requesting comfort for myself, only for help for others or to ask what else I could do for Him. But I was in such distress that I got out of bed, got on my knees, and asked, "God, will you help me?" I didn't expect anything to happen, but I was desperate. I remember that it was very quiet, and I began to feel a sense of peacefulness. Then I heard a voice somewhere inside me. The voice was calm, authoritative, kind, and much more solid than my internal voice. I knew it was Him! I heard Him say, *Do you want to learn about having peace, My child?* I held still, afraid He would go away. Then I said, "Yes!" and immediately, this vision flashed in my mind. I was standing at the very edge of a cliff. There was chaos all around me—noise, wind, rain, and lightning from a terrible storm. Then I became aware that I was totally protected. He was there too. Much taller than I was, He was standing directly behind me. His arms were wings, so large they were as tall as He was, and He was wrapping me up in them. They folded around me like a cloak. I was fully covered except for a small peephole where the wings overlapped. I felt warm and completely safe. As I watched from my peephole, I could see everything around me was being destroyed. The turmoil hit the wings, but I was untouched and at peace. It was wonderful! I asked how I could keep this peace, and He said, *Child, if you want My peace, learn to continually abide in My love. Life is full of turmoil. If I am your*

As you finish this chapter, reflect on how God is actively working on your behalf.

refuge, you will experience peace. Then the vision disappeared, and I was left with total calm and an assurance that no matter what happened He would take care of me. I have never forgotten the safety I felt wrapped up in Him that night.

Small-Group Discussion Questions

Relying only on our strength, carrying big burdens, fighting battles all alone. Many of us know how to do this well. Discuss your reactions to this chapter. What feelings did it stir up in you?

- When have you longed to be rescued but felt that no one was there to help you?

- Now, as you look back, can you see evidence of His hand in it?

- Share your song of praise with the group.

# Journaling

Write to God about any ways you feel differently about yourself or Him after working through this chapter.

_____

_____

_____

_____

_____

_____

_____

_____

_____

_____

_____

_____

_____

_____

_____

_____

_____

_____

GOD IS WORKING ON OUR BEHALF

5

God Will Always Be Faithful to Us

"I am the one who will never abandon you."

Carol's Story

In our church youth group I got labeled as a troublemaker. It was true that I didn't always follow all the rules, but any time there was a problem, I was the first person they suspected. Eventually I was asked to leave the group for something I didn't have anything to do with. They assumed it was me and wouldn't believe me when I told them it wasn't. It still makes me mad when I think about it. They rejected me unfairly and failed to understand that as a new Christian I needed a chance to grow.

I feel unfairly judged a lot in my marriage, too. When we are in conflict, my husband accuses me of not caring or not trying to make our marriage work. My reaction is to withdraw even more. I'm doing the best I can, but it's never enough. Sometimes I want to give up and be bad just because that's how he views me.

I guess I expect God to deal unfairly with me, too. I don't expect Him to intervene for me the same way He does for others. For some reason they get something I don't. It seems like He is willing to rescue them but not me. It's hard to understand why He does what He does. So I hold Him at arm's length to try and protect myself from being hurt. Needing Him too much is too big a risk. I want to make sure that I don't become too dependent on Him because He is so unpredictable.

 Journaling

What happens to our image of God when people have been unfaithful or unfair, when they have judged us carelessly, dismissed our needs, or treated us as though we were irrelevant? How can we relate to God as a faithful protector when important people would not or could not stand up for us? We want so much to believe that He will be different, but our hearts wince when we attempt to step out in faith, and we brace ourselves for betrayal. Even those in our lives now who are trying to love us fail us from time to time. They are not always able to be what we need. We keep waiting for Prince Charming to ride in on his white horse, defend our honor, and carry us off into the sunset, but he never shows up. We are left protecting ourselves, angry with those around us for not taking a risk for us—and perhaps angry with God for not saving us from harm.

> *God is just: He will pay back trouble to those who trouble you and give relief to you who are troubled.*
>
> (2 THESSALONIANS 1:6–7)

> *"I will repay you for the years the locusts have eaten—the great locust and the young locust." (JOEL 2:25)*

Who do you wish would face consequences for their unfair or unkind treatment of you?

_____

_____

_____

_____

_____

Write about the feelings that come up when you think about this.

_____

_____

_____

_____

_____

_____

Write about the consequences you have had to live with because of their sin against you, how you may have felt consumed by sadness or anger because of this situation.

_____

_____

_____

_____

_____

"God is our refuge and strength, an ever-present help in trouble. Therefore we will not fear, though the earth give way and the mountains fall into the heart of the sea, though its waters roar and foam and the mountains quake with their surging. . . . God is within her, she will not fall; God will help her at break of day."
PSALM 46:1–3, 5

Ask God to talk to you about how He has or will "repay you for the years the locusts have eaten."

_____

_____

_____

_____

The Israelites faced a huge enemy, the Anakites. They were strong and tall and seemingly undefeatable. Like the Israelites, we are often intimidated by strong forces in our lives. It may be a relationship that feels impossible to put back together or a behavior that seems in control of us. But the Anakites are not too much for our Protector. He says He will go ahead of us and fight for us—like a devouring fire!

> *Hear, O Israel. You are now about to cross the Jordan to go in and dispossess nations greater and stronger than you, with large cities that have walls up to the sky. The people are strong and tall—Anakites! . . . But be assured today that the LORD your God is the one who goes across ahead of you like a devouring fire. He will destroy them; he will subdue them before you. And you will drive them out and annihilate them quickly, as the LORD has promised you.* (DEUTERONOMY 9:1–3)

Who or what in your life feels too "strong and tall" for you to overcome? Who or what do you feel you cannot stand up against (your self-doubt, self-contempt, an abusive person, a bondage you are struggling to free yourself from)? Talk to God about this struggle.

_____

_____

_____

_____

_____

_____

_____

_____

Ask God to show you how He will subdue this force in your life. Write down what you experience.

_____

_____

_____

_____

_____

_____

Then I said to you, "Do not be terrified; do not be afraid of them. The LORD your God, who is going before you, will fight for you, as he did for you in Egypt, before your very eyes, and in the desert. There you saw how the LORD your God carried you, as a father carries his son, all the way you went until you reached this place."

In spite of this, you did not trust in the LORD your God, who went ahead of you on your journey.

(DEUTERONOMY 1:29–33)

Moses answered the people, "Do not be afraid. Stand firm and you will see the deliverance the LORD will bring you today. The Eqyptians you see today you will never see again. The LORD will fight for you; you need only to be still."

(EXODUS 14:13–14)

The one who calls you is faithful and he will do it.

(1 THESSALONIANS 5:24)

Reflect on a specific area where you would like God to go ahead of you and fight for you. Write about how big this issue seems to you and share your feelings about it with God.

_____

_____

_____

_____

_____

_____

_____

Now speak to Him about why previously you have not believed He could carry you on this journey.

_____

_____

_____

_____

_____

Imagine yourself on this journey with God, with Him carrying you every step of the way, "as a father carries his son, all the way you went until you reached this place." How is He carrying you? What is He guarding you against along the way?

_____

_____

_____

_____

_____

_____

What does it mean to you when He says in His Word "He will do it"?
Talk to Him about this, and then take some time to listen to what He has
to say.

_____

_____

_____

_____

_____

⤚ Kelly's Story ⤙

*When I was a little girl, I adored my daddy. Even when he and my
mother divorced, I continued to believe in him. Over time, however, I
began to see how selfish he was. First he was hours, then days late for
visits with me. Eventually he didn't even show up on weekends he had
promised to spend with me. It was so painful to realize I had given him
my heart and it was of no value to him.*

*I've had the same experience in my marriage. When my husband
and I were dating, we broke up because he was unfaithful to me. I was
done with the relationship, but he continued to pursue me, and as time
went by I began to feel God changing my heart toward him. After several years of marriage I found out that he was having an affair and
struggling with a sexual addiction. I felt like God had set me up. He
knew that this man would betray me, but He had allowed me to open*

up to him again and to marry him. I felt fooled. I had given my heart
again to someone who was untrustworthy.

I am so afraid that God can't be trusted either. Intellectually I
know that's not true, but I can't seem to get past the fear that really
giving myself to Him means I'm in for more betrayal. I don't know how
to believe that my needs will be important to Him. I feel like our rela-
tionship is about me being there to do what He wants me to do, but I
don't expect Him to take care of me in a way that makes me feel safe
and valued. ❧

Journaling

Being abandoned or betrayed by a significant person in your life leaves a huge wound. Sometimes it feels like it can never be healed, like you will always live with questions about why you weren't enough to stay for, enough to be true to. Isaiah encourages us to hear that the Father is a faithful rescuer. He wants us to know that while deep waters may threaten us, they will not sweep over us; though the fire may come, we will not be burned. He will be with us.

> *But now, this is what the LORD says—he who created you, O*
> *Jacob, he who formed you, O Israel: "Fear not, for I have*
> *redeemed you; I have summoned you by name; you are mine.*
> *When you pass through the waters, I will be with you; and*

when you pass through the rivers, they will not sweep over you. When you walk through the fire, you will not be burned; the flames will not set you ablaze. For I am the LORD, your God, the Holy One of Israel, your Savior; I give Egypt for your ransom, Cush and Seba in your stead. Since you are precious and honored in my sight, and because I love you, I will give men in exchange for you, and people in exchange for your life. Do not be afraid, for I am with you." (ISAIAH 43:1–5)

He reached down from on high and took hold of me; he drew me out of deep waters. He rescued me from my powerful enemy, from my foes, who were too strong for me. They confronted me in the day of my disaster, but the LORD was my support. He brought me out into a spacious place; he rescued me because he delighted in me. (PSALM 18:16–19)

Ask God to lead you through the following questions. Imagine God's hands gripping yours, drawing you out of deep, drowning waters. What do you feel like in this moment? What thoughts are running through your head?

Now imagine that you are being miraculously lifted out of the consuming waters, that you can look back and see your "powerful enemy, your foes" pursuing you during your rescue. What or who are they? What are they doing in this moment?

_____

_____

_____

_____

Now picture yourself in a "spacious place." What does this place look like? What feelings are you aware of in this place? Where is God?

_____

_____

_____

_____

_____

God rescued you because He delighted in you. Take a moment to listen to Him tell you why He delights in you. Don't be embarrassed if it sounds silly to write these things about yourself. He wants you to know and believe in your heart that He delights in you. You are worth rescuing!

_____

_____

_____

_____

_____

Some wandered in desert wastelands, finding no way to a city where they could settle. They were hungry and thirsty, and their lives ebbed away. Then they cried out to the LORD in their trouble, and he delivered them from their distress. He led them by a straight way to a city where they could settle. Let them give thanks to the LORD for his unfailing love and his wonderful deeds for men, for he satisfies the thirsty and fills the hungry with good things. (PSALM 107:4–9)

For the LORD your God is bringing you into a good land—a land with streams and pools of water, with springs flowing in the valleys and hills; a land with wheat and barley, vines and fig trees, pomegranates, olive oil and honey; a land where bread will not be scarce and you will lack nothing; a land where the rocks are iron and you can dig copper out of the hills. (DEUTERONOMY 8:7–9)

What "good things" would fill you? What would you imagine your life looking like if you were to lack nothing?

_____

_____

_____

_____

_____

Ask God to talk to you about the good things He wishes to give you, the kind of contentment He wants you to know.

_____

_____

_____

_____

_____

Experiences with God

Olivia's Experience

I was standing in the shower one day in despair. My husband and I were really struggling. Our marriage had been limping through a huge crisis, and I wasn't sure our relationship could survive it—or even if I wanted it to. Months before, I had clearly felt that God had directed me to face the fear of this pain and allow Him to restore our relationship. But we had had a couple of bad days—situations where I thought my husband once again ignored my concerns and dismissed my feelings. I got into the shower to get away from everyone. I was crying and thinking about how abandoned and foolish I felt for continuing to try to make this relationship work. I was overwhelmed with how impossible it seemed. I was saying, "God, where are You, where are You?" Then my daughter, who was five at the time, climbed in the shower with me. I was barely aware of her presence until I heard her softly singing a song I had never heard her sing before:

"He didn't bring us this far to leave us.
He didn't teach us to swim to let us drown.
He didn't build His home in us to move away.
He didn't bring us up to let us down."

There He was! In that moment, God's presence so clearly broke into my despair through my daughter's sweet little voice. It was as if He held me in the shower, comforting me as I cried, reminding me that He was still there and still working. Even though things weren't going well, even though things looked hopeless, He was there, and He would make a way. I will never forget how nurtured I felt by Him that day.

Jeannie's Experience

At midlife, I'd lost the joy in my life. I began to work with a Christian therapist because of stress and depression after becoming my parents' caregiver. Being thrust into this role opened up a myriad of feelings that I hadn't connected with before. At the same time I felt dead inside and uninterested in the day-to-day. I began to identify for the first time that I was never nurtured, developed, or really cared for. I still felt like the ugly ducking, the unblessed child of the family. My picture and experience of God was of a distant inspector. I had lost hope of ever being cared for. My mind and heart concluded that life was about fulfilling my duties, and that aching and longing for love was silliness. By now I had become immune from feeling much of anything about anyone, including God.

During the process of closing my parents' home of fifty years, I inherited a lonely dog. She was an extraordinarily well-bred creature—athletic, smart, and sensitive. And absolutely neglected. My older brother had bought Jesse on a whim, dumped her with my parents, leaving her alone when they moved to a nursing home. Without proper care, she had become wild and anxious. I brought her home and committed myself to loving her. I took her on long walks every day, signed her up for obedience training, bought her a special ID tag, put up a new fence to keep her safe. Before long she became calm and happy, finally secure.

As I was discussing the acquisition of the dog with my counselor, he noticed a parallel between my feelings toward Jesse and God's feelings toward me. He said that the way I was investing in the dog—loving her, helping her—was a picture of how God wants to invest in, love, and develop me. With my customary cynicism, I took his perspective with a grain of salt. He also suggested I journal about the process unfolding between me and the dog and view it as a picture of God and me. Dutifully I journaled. I wrote a paragraph pointing out that my investment in Jesse's safety, training, play, and boundaries might (somehow) be a parallel to God's intentions toward me. I closed the journal, put on my hiking boots, and left the house to hike with some friends.

A few minutes into our walk, we released our dogs from their leashes so they could play and explore alongside the trail. They never wandered out of earshot or eyesight. Until suddenly Jesse wasn't there. I called her, casually at first. Then I became frantic, realizing she was lost. We searched. We backtracked. We called her name over and over. Shame washed over me. How could I be so careless? What will I tell everyone? Then I was seized with my affection for Jesse. I loved her! I wanted her back. I wanted to be with her. She was my sweet dog. I had paid a price for her. I had poured time and energy into her, and I wanted her back.

The search proved futile. We made our way back down the trail to a nearby veterinarian's office to check if they had any information about a lost dog. It turned out that another hiker had found Jesse and taken her home, leaving a name and phone number with the veterinarian. I was so relieved. I raced home to call the woman, but there was no answer. We traced the name and number to a specific address in Denver, twenty miles down the highway from our little mountain town. Why did she take Jesse so far away? Over and over throughout the day I tried to reach her. Still no answer. I began to fear that the stranger would keep Jesse and never return her. So I decided to go get her. I drove down the mountain and found the woman's house. It turned out that my worst fears were true! It was clear when I got there that the woman was not planning to return my calls. She was already pretending Jesse was hers. But I got Jesse back. I was relentless in my pursuit, and it had paid off.

I came home, exhausted from the stress of the entire experience. As I sat quietly and retraced the events of the day, the words of my counselor came to mind . . . "Your feelings for Jesse are just a sliver of God's feelings for you." Even against my typically cynical mind, the truth was undeniable. All my over-the-top feelings and efforts on behalf of Jesse in the last few hours were exactly how God pursues me. My journaling about it just before it happened was no accident. God wanted me to see that He comes after me in the same way. He loves me this much! I got this visual image of God running after me, His voice echoing all over the creation, pursuing me. He is doing it with abandon and compelling purpose. Yet I can't hear Him because I am coursing and whirling, not staying in one place. Jesse's behavior gave me such a clear picture of my own. If Jesse had stopped and been still along the trail, I would have found her in the first hour. But her thrashing led her to false safety—the stranger who took her home. It gave her partial relief but an uneasy rest.

> "They will fight against you but will not overcome you, for I am with you and will rescue you," declares the LORD.
> JEREMIAH 1:19

 I pick substitutes for God, too. People or material things may meet my needs temporarily, but the feeling of security they bring doesn't last. I usually guard my heart with my mind. I prevent experiences from getting to me. I reason them out. I gain my view of God only from cognitive sources—Scripture, teaching, and reason. I dislike the sentimental and am suspicious of my heart or my gut instincts. Yet from this powerful, exhausting experience, I received a tangible visual of God's love for me. He passionately pursues me because He wants me. He is looking for me, calling my name, even before I know I'm lost. Even when I'm disoriented and may think He has forgotten me, He is acting to retrieve me. He wants me to feel it. He wants this encounter to stick with me. He wants me to know that I'm as loved and lovable as Jesse and that He will not give me up.

Grace's Experience

I had awakened around 3:00, early Christmas morning, my soul in despair, my heart heavy. The past few months had been turbulent and painful. I was struggling in my marriage, struggling in my heart, struggling in nearly every area of my life. I felt alone, tired, weary. By faith I knew that God had not abandoned me. Yet in the past turbulent, painful days the Prince of Peace had seemed silent. And distant. I could not see His face, or hear His voice, or reach out to touch Him.

Praise Me, His still, small voice broke through the silence. As I lay there in the dark, the snow beginning to fall, I allowed myself to think of all the reasons I had to praise Him. Then faces began to appear in my mind. Faces of people I loved and who loved me. Faces of those I rejoiced with and wept with. Faces of those who had wounded me and whom I had wounded. I praised Him for these people in my life.

Then gently, one by one, the Lord gave those faces back to me. Of the first two women He said tenderly, *These are My face to you. The love you see in their eyes, the tender looks, the tears and the laughter expressed to you—these are a glimpse of My face and the love I feel for you.* Of the next two friends He said, *These are My hands that have served you. When you were too weak, to weary to go on, they have been My hands of service for you. They have helped you do the things you could not do on your own.* Of one He explained, *She is My righteous anger for you. She is angry over the wrongs committed against you. So am I.* Of another, *She is My Word, spoken to you.* Other faces were those filled with His Spirit in prayer, interceding His will for my life. At last He came to those people whom I praised Him for by faith. Their sins have cut deep, my wounds often raw. Of one He showed me her unwillingness to yield to Him, of her inability to sit still, be quiet, and let Him heal her. I heard His voice say to me, *Be still, and know that I am God. Come to Me, and I will give you rest. If you do not, like her, your scars will remain. It takes time to rebuild. It takes time to rise up.* Of the last one, most important of all, He said, *You have made his words an idol in your mind. You have put the lies of shame and self-hatred, failure and unworthiness above the truth of what I say about you. I have called you* beloved. *I chose you before the foundations of the world. Your name is inscribed on the palm of My hand.*

As you finish this chapter, reflect on how God will always be faithful to you.

God was gently calling me to repent, for I had worshiped lies instead of His truth, deception instead of His righteousness. Captivity instead of freedom and mercy and grace. He had not forsaken me. Rather, my king and my Lord came down on that holy night to reveal Himself once more in His abundant love. He came unexpectedly—in power and in hope. He came in tenderness and conviction. As He showed me His face, His heart, His hands, His truth,

I felt His peace wash over me. It was a feeling of quiet strength. My circumstances hadn't changed. I knew the day ahead would be filled with more struggle. Yet I felt different somehow, no longer so alone.

Small-Group Discussion Questions

We've been talking about how God is not afraid of your wrestling with Him on painful issues. He will not leave you. And even if you try to leave Him, He will pull out all the stops to bring you back.

- Talk about the struggle between your heart and your head. Your head knows He is faithful, but sometimes your heart is afraid He will not be faithful specifically to you. Share these feelings with the group.

- What are some areas of your life where you would like to see God fight for you?

- Describe your spacious place from your journaling on page 111.

Journaling

Write to God about any ways you feel differently about yourself or Him after working through this chapter.

_____

_____

_____

_____

_____

_____

_____

_____

_____

_____

_____

_____

_____

_____

_____

_____

_____

_____

_____

GOD WILL ALWAYS BE FAITHFUL TO US

6

God Believes in Who
He Created Us to Be

"I am the one who believes in you."

Diana's Story

Things never seemed to work out for our family. My dad became disabled when we were young, and my mom had to support the family. Life was such a struggle for them. Whenever they attempted to pursue a dream they had, things fell apart. They would get excited about some possibility, but somehow it would never happen. Their dreams never came true. They didn't have hope for themselves, and they passed on that hopelessness to us. My dad, especially, had low expectations for his life and for us, and we all met those expectations. We were major low achievers. We never learned to persevere.

I've always dropped out of things. I dropped out of college when I was close to graduating and still haven't finished. I guess I don't expect to complete things or be successful so I don't push through when things get hard. I don't think much about what could be or what I might want for myself. I learned that there's no point in dreaming because things don't work out.

I don't think of God as having any plans for my life either. I don't see myself as essential to His work because I don't think I'm capable of contributing in a significant way. I know that I'm good at some things but not at anything that makes a difference in people's lives.

Journaling

Some of us have lost hope that our lives will ever amount to much. We are so out of touch with any dreams we may have once had for ourselves that we can't even remember them. Instead we have adjusted to the idea that we will never be anything special, never succeed where we presently experience failure. We've let go of the hope that God will ever use us in meaningful ways. Rather, we've decided we ought to just be grateful for the good we do have. Wishing, hoping for more is pie in the sky.

> *I remember my affliction and my wandering, the bitterness and the gall. I well remember them, and my soul is downcast within me. Yet this I call to mind and therefore I have hope: Because of the LORD's great love we are not consumed, for his compassions never fail. They are new every morning; great is your faithfulness. I say to myself, "The LORD is my portion; therefore I will wait for him." (LAMENTATIONS 3:19–24)*

What are you waiting on God for?

_____

_____

_____

_____

_____

Is there someone in your life you could share this with who will be hopeful for you? Consider asking that person to pray regularly for you or even with you about this issue.

_____

_____

_____

_____

_____

_____

_____

But the pot he was shaping from the clay was marred in his hands; so the potter formed it into another pot, shaping it as seemed best to him.

Then the word of the LORD came to me: "O house of Israel, can I not do with you as this potter does?" declares the LORD. "Like clay in the hand of the potter, so are you in my hand, O house of Israel." (JEREMIAH 18:4–6)

How has your life been stretched in difficult ways by the Potter? What has He allowed in your life that created pain or loss?

_____

_____

_____

_____

_____

_____

_____

_____

How has God used these hurts in your life? What are some of the things
He has shown you through them?

_____

_____

_____

_____

_____

_____

_____

Ask God to show you how He is shaping you today. Listen for His voice.
Allow Him to soothe you with the truth of how He is actively molding
and shaping you.

_____

_____

_____

_____

_____

_____

Jennifer's Story

I wanted to be respected by my dad so badly that I pretended to be another person for him. I knew he wouldn't approve of who I really was, so I tried to be the kind of person he would be proud of. Hearing him talk about other people let me know what I needed to avoid being. He seemed to approve of this person I had made up, so I kept up the act. When I got pregnant and had an abortion, I knew it was something I would need to keep secret. He was very critical of others, and I had heard him talk about what losers women were who had abortions. Being around him was miserable because of my fear of being found out.

It's been hard for me to be real with other people in my life, too. I'm afraid that if I stop pretending to be what I am supposed to be, there will be no one there to love me. Withholding the truth of my life seems normal to me. I can avoid being rejected if I can just figure out what people want from me.

In my relationship with God this comes up big-time. I'm always comparing myself with others to help me figure out if I'm valuable to Him. Now that my husband and I are struggling with infertility, I feel judged by God, as if He is saying I'm not doing a good enough job with the child I have, so why would He give me another? I compare myself with women who have more children and try to prove to myself that I don't deserve this judgment from Him, that He made a mistake. Then I try to make myself more valuable to God in hopes that if I am more worthy of His love, maybe He'll remove this judgment from me. I

know that none of this is true about God's dealings with us, but I struggle with these feelings a lot. ～

Journaling

Pretending is so easy. It's what most people want from us. They want us to say we're fine, we're content and happy, we have no doubts about God's dealings in our lives or in the lives of those we love. Voicing our disappointments or hopelessness can be perceived as a lack of belief, as spiritual immaturity, when it often reveals an intense desire to know God in a deeper way. Holding on to hope that He will work can sometimes be a fight.

> *"I will go before you and will level the mountains; I will break down gates of bronze and cut through bars of iron. I will give you the treasures of darkness, riches stored in secret places, so that you may know that I am the LORD, the God of Israel, who summons you by name." (ISAIAH 45:2–3)*

> *Many, O LORD my God, are the wonders you have done. The things you planned for us no one can recount to you; were I to speak and tell of them, they would be too many to declare.* (Psalm 40:5)

What are some of your dreams for the future? In what ways do you desire to see God move in the next few years?

_____

_____

_____

_____

_____

What mountains would God need to level to make these dreams a reality?

_____

_____

_____

_____

Experiences with God

Juli's Experience

Today I read this passage:

> *Jesus, once more deeply moved, came to the tomb. It was a cave with a stone laid across the entrance. "Take away the stone," he said.*

"But, Lord," said Martha, the sister of the dead man, "by this time there is a bad odor, for he has been there four days."

Then Jesus said, "Did I not tell you that if you believed, you would see the glory of God?"

So they took away the stone. Then Jesus looked up and said, "Father, I thank you that you have heard me. I knew that you always hear me, but I said this for the benefit of the people standing here, that they may believe that you sent me."

When he had said this, Jesus called in a loud voice, "Lazarus, come out!" The dead man came out, his hands and feet wrapped with strips of linen, and a cloth around his face.

Jesus said to them, "Take off the grave clothes and let him go." (JOHN 11:38–44)

"You are a chosen people, a royal priesthood, a holy nation, a people belonging to God, that you may declare the praises of him who called you out of darkness into his wonderful light."
1 PETER 2:9

As I read this I heard God's Spirit say somewhere deep inside me, *You are like Lazarus.* I have been dead for a long time. I am bound by burial clothes, filthy rags that I have been clothed in for so long. But I think You are calling me forth from the grave, out of my stench and darkness into Your light. The cave I have been unwilling to leave is dark and filthy, musty and cold. But I have been here a long time—I can control it. I know it well. I have learned to survive here. But You, Lord, are standing—and waiting—right outside this cave. I am terrified. What is on the other side of the stone? Do I dare hope that You will be there, with joy and newness of life? Is there death outside, or are You there, patiently waiting for me to place my trust in Your care? You call me to come. But I am afraid. Can I trust You to see me through? As I read this story again, I feel clearer that these words are for me. By faith I want to come toward You and allow You to help me as You desire. I know You've placed people in my life to help me take this step. Lord, let me trust them. Help me believe that You will not leave me. You will breathe new life into my being.

Katherine's Experience

Last night when I got home from my group, my heart was heavy. I felt overwhelmed with my friends' hurts, my hurts, the reality that my relationship with You doesn't feel intimate. I feel tired, alone, desiring more in my relationship with You, with others. Am I missing the whole point somehow? I've tasted that high of feeling close to You. Then somehow I lose it—the feeling fades, and I'm back to feeling disconnected. This morning I was leafing through the Word when a subtitle caught my attention. It was Isaiah 35, the "Joy of the Redeemed." As I read the opening verses I was struck by this picture of what You desire for me.

> "For I know the plans I have for you," declares the LORD, "plans to prosper you and not to harm you, plans to give you a hope and a future."
> Jeremiah 29:11

The desert and the parched land will be glad; the wilderness will rejoice and blossom. Like the crocus, it will burst into bloom. (ISAIAH 35:1–2)

In so many ways, I have been a desert. Some flowers are in bloom, there is some evidence of Your life in me, but the majority of my land is a little parched, barren, feeling untouched by You. How can I feel this way? I've been a Christian for a long time, but it is clear I'm not experiencing the joy of the redeemed. You desire blooms, beautiful flowers throughout the land—throughout me. Then I read on.

Then will the eyes of the blind be opened and the ears of the deaf unstopped. Then will the lame leap like a deer, and the mute tongue shout for joy. Water will gush forth in the wilderness and streams in the desert. (ISAIAH 35:5–6)

As you finish this chapter, reflect on how God believes in you.

I am burdened with negative perceptions about myself that make me lame. These thoughts taunt me, preventing me from feeling redeemed. Whispers in my ear say, "You're not a good enough friend, mother, wife, Christian . . . " They keep me stuck, lame, disconnected from You. But after reading these verses I can picture myself leaping like a deer, free and strong—unhindered by these voices from Satan that keep me in bondage, blind and mute. You have shown me such a beautiful picture of Your vision for my life. It is life—full and abundant, teeming with wildlife and beautiful flowers. Thank You for this picture. I pray it will become truth for me.

Small-Group Discussion Questions

Ask someone in the group to read Isaiah 61:1–4. Close your eyes and listen to God's words of hope for you.

- Talk about where you see God's restoring hand in your past or present.

- Share how you see God working to create strength and beauty in each other. Go around the circle, sharing about each person.

- As each person shares her thoughts about you, write down what you are hearing. Later, take some time to reflect on what others see in you. Let their words sink in. Trust them to speak truth to you.

Journaling

Write to Him about any ways you feel differently about yourself or Him after working through this chapter.

_____

_____

_____

_____

_____

_____

_____

_____

_____

_____

_____

_____

_____

_____

_____

_____

_____

_____

_____

7

God Will Continue to Pursue Us

"I will not let go of you."

God is continually wooing us, inviting us to embrace a full and abundant relationship with Him. But we often run. It's easier to be emotionally dead, cut off from our longings. Then things stay manageable. We don't expect much from God, so we are never in touch with our desperation for Him. We can live a controlled, predicable life. He stays inside His box, and we stay inside ours.

But our desire for you in this journey is that you choose life, choose to wrestle with God. This process can be messy, that is assured. Sometimes you will have to think about and feel things you don't want to. Sometimes you will have to argue with God about things you don't understand. Sometimes you will have to go through the valley, where things are lonely and hard. But if you make the journey, you will experience new freedom and richness, and an abundance of life you've never known before, deep and satisfying.

(Kathy) Sometimes He shows up in mysterious ways—when we least expect it. During the process of writing this book, God used my daughter, Julia, to teach me something big about my relationship with Him. We had just had her parent-teacher conference. Things were going great for her, but there was one area that her teacher wanted her to work on—participating in class more. Thinking this was no big deal, I reviewed her report card with her. Then I mentioned her teacher's concern. I was stunned by Julia's reaction! She completely lost it. She burst into tears, crying, "What more do you want from me? I'm trying as hard as I can. . . . I don't understand how

I can do more! I DO participate! I AM trying!" Those words cut deep into my heart, and I realized in that moment how it felt for her to have one more thing heaped on her shoulders. She had already stretched herself, and it still wasn't enough.

At the end of our conversation, Julia was exhausted and quiet. Finally, after quite a while, she murmured softly, "I just want you to hold me. I just want you to love me." Overwhelmed with care and concern for her, I gathered her up in my lap and held her. I stroked her hair and told her over and over, "I love you. You don't have to do one more thing. You are precious just like you are."

The next morning I was still troubled by how familiar Julia's feelings were. I got on the computer to journal about this experience and wrestle with the way I share Julia's frustration. Oh, I know this is a picture of me! I feel the same feelings. I fall apart sometimes, too, when I can't meet everyone's expectations. I hear their unsatisfied voices, demanding more than I can give. Then I feel tired. And I want to plead with God, "Why is all I do not enough?" I feel all alone, and I want to turn to Him, but I'm afraid He shares the same expectations. I'm doing everything I know how to do, and I want to argue with God, "What more do You want from me?"

It was so natural for Julia to receive my comfort. But I struggle to ask my heavenly Father to hold me, and yet it's exactly what I need. To rest in His arms and have Him say, "It's okay. There's nothing more you need to do."

During my journaling time, I reflected on this situation and poured out my feelings about it to God. As I sat at the computer sharing my heart with Him, I felt His presence strongly. These words flowed out, His words for me: *Oh, darling, you don't need to do more. I want you to know you are loved just as you are. You need not do anything different to please Me. You only need to rest here. Let Me help you. Let Me fill you with My Spirit so that you are clear about who you are in Me. That is where your strength comes from. You are complete in Me! You are worthy. Do you hear Me, My daughter, YOU ARE WORTHY! I love you with a love that can't be changed. That can't be lost. Keep coming to Me, longing for Me, tasting My fruit, eating food from My table that fills you up and leaves you satisfied.*

With tears streaming down my face, I knew He was impressing a deep, important truth into my heart. In that moment I gained a clearer understanding of who I was in His eyes. I wrote to Him, "Thank You, Lord. Thank You! I am so grateful for this time when I really heard You. I am worthy. It is enough. You are enough. I am enough."

Journaling

Evaluate your journey through this workbook. Take some time to step back and examine where you are now.

- ❧ Which chapters did you relate to most?

- ❧ What has God changed in you over the course of this material?

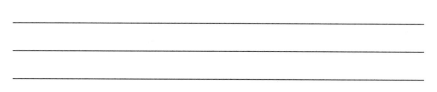

_____

_____

_____

_____

_____

_____

_____

_____

_____

_____

_____

_____

_____

_____

_____

❧ Where do you want God to continue to speak to you? Use
the checklist below to help clarify.

I long to know more deeply that God . . .

    ❑ loves me regardless of my performance.

    ❑ wants to be involved in the intimate details of my life.

    ❑ is actively working on my behalf, rescuing, restoring.

    ❑ will not pull the rug out from under me.

    ❑ believes in who He created me to be.

    ❑ will pursue me until I can trust Him.

    ❑ is not afraid of my desperation to be truly loved.

Your Experiences with God

How has God been showing up in your life? Describe those experiences on the following page. How did they change your view of Him? Of yourself? When you are done, share it with your group or some friends to solidify the truth that God wants you to hear. We'd love to hear about it, too! E-mail your experience to Out of the Mud Ministries. Our e-mail address is: outofthemud@juno.com

God is not afraid that you still have struggles, that you have not arrived. The purpose of this material was to open the door of your heart to a deeper, more powerful relationship with Him. Our hope is that you will keep the door open. He is not afraid of your desperation. He is big enough, strong enough for your stuff. He can handle it. He wants to handle it. He wants to show up in your life, to make Himself tangible. Look for Him. As we shared in the beginning, connecting with God on this emotional level takes practice. It is not something to be mastered but a process to be embraced. Keep talking to Him about your fears. Keep inviting Him into the deepest spaces of your heart. It's where He wants to go!

"Arise, come, my darling; my beautiful one, come with me."
(SONG OF SONGS 2:13)